THE
BETTA FISH
Complete Guide

ISBN: 9798862008258

Immersion in a
fascinating world

A number of scientific studies have shown that contemplating an aquarium has many benefits, not least in reducing daily stress. Observing this reconstituted piece of nature in a corner of your living room, office or bedroom can literally relax and soothe you. It can also elegantly decorate a room, bringing life and color to it.

But all this only works if some basic rules are observed: proper care and rigorous maintenance to meet the needs of your fighter and the plants in your aquarium. Otherwise, this fantastic ecosystem could quickly turn into a nightmare for you and your fish...

In this step-by-step guide to fighting fish, we'll see together how to create the aquarium of your dreams, while respecting the fundamental rules of aquaristics.

Introduction

The aim of this guide is to provide you with all the information and knowledge necessary to start your cohabitation with your new scaled companion in the best possible way.

Siamese fighting fish have become iconic fish. True models of our aquariums, fascinating both young and old, novice aquarists and seasoned experts alike. Unfortunately, their popularity does not increase in the same way as the understanding of their needs. Even today, many false beliefs remain about them and it is still too common to see fighter fish kept in neglected or even aberrant conditions.

In this book, we will review all the important aspects of betta fish care. We will begin with a detailed presentation of these fish, focusing particularly on the Betta splendens species, which is the most common variety found in aquariums. We'll explore their origin, natural habitat, lifestyle, behavior, and character to help you understand and best meet all of their needs.

Next, we'll examine the aquarium setup from a technical perspective : shape, dimensions, location, equipment, layout, decorations, and more. We'll thoroughly analyze all these elements to ensure your future betta feels right at home!

Finally, we'll cover reception and maintenance: how to properly cycle an aquarium (nitrogen cycle), how to choose your fish, how to acclimate it, how to feed it, how to maintain your aquarium, and how to quickly detect signs of discomfort or disease in order to address them as promptly as possible.

So, let's dive in and get started !

SUMMARY

The betta fish

Presentation and origin

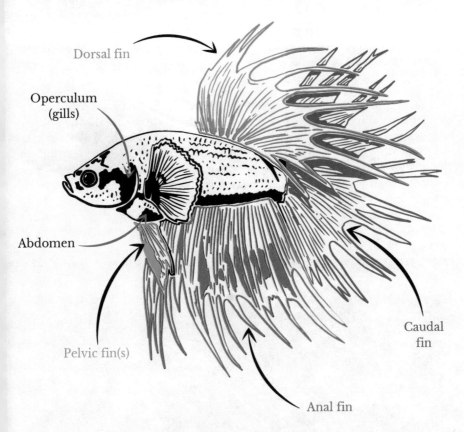

Dorsal fin

Operculum (gills)

Abdomen

Pelvic fin(s)

Caudal fin

Anal fin

Commonly called "Betta" or "Siamese fighting fish", these names reflect the origins of this small fish from Southeast Asia. Originally bred in Thailand (formerly the region known as the Kingdom of Siam), its aggressive and territorial temperament towards its own species and certain other aquatic species in confined spaces earned it the reputation of a fighter. Two males together being able to fight and kill each other until death.

For over 500 years, Betta fish have been bred for the purpose of organizing fights. This practice continues to this day in their country of origin, where betting on the winners of these contests still occurs.

While the practice of fish fighting still exists in some places, the breeding of Betta splendens (its scientific name) has largely shifted towards a less barbaric and more aesthetic pursuit. Through extensive breeding and genetic selection, breeders have succeeded in developing individuals with vibrant, varied colors and fins of incredible sizes and shapes. This diversity in appearance is largely responsible for the betta's popularity in aquariums ! Today, betta fish can be found in almost all pet stores, and many enthusiasts around the world dedicate themselves to breeding these fish. Due to their hardiness, diverse shapes / colors and generally low purchase cost, bettas have become a go-to choice for many first-time fish owners (rivaling goldfish in popularity).

When properly cared for and their needs are met, betta fish can be delightful companions, providing years of enjoyment through their observation. On average, a Betta splendens has a lifespan of 2 to 4 years in an aquarium. This duration can be extended or shortened depending on the quality of life the fish experiences. Some individuals have been known to live more than 5 years ! It's important to note that while bettas are often considered "easy" pets, their longevity and health are directly tied to the quality of care they receive. Proper tank size, water quality, diet and overall environment play crucial roles in ensuring a betta's well-being and maximizing its lifespan.

▲ The fighter is a very curious and intelligent companion to which one quickly becomes attached.

The betta fish

Species and forms

As mentioned earlier, the betta family encompasses a wide variety of individuals with diverse physical characteristics and behaviors. The term "betta" actually refers to multiple species, and there are more than 75 species divided into 13 complexes or varieties!

Among these 13 complexes, the Splendens complex is of particular interest. This complex itself includes 6 subspecies of Betta, with Betta splendens being the one we're primarily focused on in this guide.

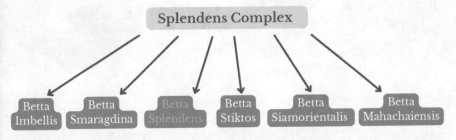

Splendens Complex

Betta Imbellis — Betta Smaragdina — Betta Splendens — Betta Stiktos — Betta Siamorientalis — Betta Mahachaiensis

The *Betta splendens* subspecies itself exhibits significant physical variations among individuals within its species, including differences in shape, color, and size. This remarkable diversity is the result of numerous genetic selections carried out over several generations by dedicated breeders, giving us the magnificent array we see today. Many of these distinct forms have been given specific names and it's quite possible that your betta fish (or your future betta fish) belongs to one of these named varieties !

- Key points to note -

- **Genetic diversity** : The variations in Betta splendens are primarily due to selective breeding rather than natural evolution.
- **Named varieties** : Many distinct forms have been officially recognized and named by breeders and enthusiasts.
- **Physical characteristics** : The differences can be observed in various aspects such as fin shape and size, body shape and coloration.
- **Continuing evolution** : New varieties continue to emerge as breeders experiment with different genetic combinations.

Let's see now an overview of the main shapes you may encounter.

The different forms of betta splendens

Veilteil or veil tail (most common)

Recognizable by its long, drooping dorsal and caudal fins. In motion, the caudal fin is round and more or less pointed towards the end.

Halfmoon

It takes its name from its large caudal fin open at an angle of 160° to 180°. The Halfmoon shape can be combined with many other shapes (plakat, crowntail, ...).

Overhalfmoon

Similar to the Halfmoon shape, the only difference is the caudal fin which is open at an angle greater than 180°.

Plakat
(Short fins)

The plakat is the form of short-finned betta. The males thus have the same appearance as the females (in addition to colour) and are generally more active and better swimmers than the other forms with long fins.

Halfmoon plakat

Combination of plakat and halfmoon form. It has short fins but a caudal fin open more than 160°.

Spadetail
(pointed tail)

Variant of the plakat, its caudal and anal fins end in a point and are not drooping.

Crowntail

The crowntail has pointed fins giving the appearance of a crown. Its fin rays are larger than those of other forms.

Combtail

Similar in appearance to crowntails, the combtail has shorter, less pronounced peaks. The fins thus have a rather "crenellated" appearance.

Rosetail

The rosetail sports excessive branching at the caudal fin. This gives it a crumpled appearance, reminiscent of a rose.

Feathertail

The feathertail is the exaggerated shape of the rosetail with an even more crinkled and irregular tail fin edge, giving more of a feathery appearance.

Delta

Akin to a sail tail shape, delta bettas are distinguished by fins that do not fall and a caudal fin open at less than 160° with very straight and symmetrical edges.

Super delta

Similar to the delta, the super delta has a triangular tail fin, more open between 160° and 180°.

Doubletail

This form has a caudal fin divided into two lobes, ideally equal. It has a larger dorsal fin and a generally more compact body than other forms.

The betta fish

Biotope

The Betta splendens originates from Thailand and Malaysia. It is found today in its natural state in Vietnam, Cambodia and Laos and also in Latin America such as Brazil or Colombia, in the United States or in Singapore where it was introduced artificially by man and where it has adapted perfectly now. To feel good, it needs a specific biotope : slightly acidic and rather soft water, where the temperature fluctuates between 75°F and 83 °F. A weak current or even shallow stagnant water, with a large plant mass (living such as aquatic and marsh plants but also in the form of organic matter such as decomposing leaves, dead wood, roots, etc.)

▲ Type of natural habitat where betta lives

▶ In its natural environment, the betta lives in slow-flowing rivers as well as in rice fields or low-oxygenated and shallow water bodies. During dry periods, it is not uncommon for the betta fish to find itself isolated in very small volumes of water (almost dry rice paddies or even puddles). Nature, being well-designed, has equipped the betta with a unique respiratory system : a labyrinth. This organ, similar to a lung, allows it to breathe air directly from the surface in order to obtain oxygen. This adaptation is crucial for survival in its often oxygen-poor habitats.

Similarly, the betta proves to be an excellent jumper, which allows it to move easily when the water level or the conditions of its environment are no longer satisfactory. This is why it is always necessary to provide a cover on the aquarium of a betta. Failure to do so may result in finding one's fish outside the tank one day, completely dried up on the floor. This natural jumping behavior, while adaptive in the wild, can prove dangerous in a home aquarium.

ℹ Characteristics of the betta biotope :

 Low current   Lot of plants   🌡 75 - 83 °F   (pH) 6 - 7,2   (GH) 7 - 20°

The betta fish

Behavior and cohabitation

The Betta splendens is a highly territorial and solitary fish, tolerating very little the presence of other individuals of its species in its area. In addition to belligerent behavior between males that can lead to deadly fights, some individuals are also very aggressive towards females. This is why breeding among bettas can be a very complicated endeavor and should only be attempted by aquarists who are already well-experienced with this species.

However, it is not uncommon to observe males making bubble nests (normally created for breeding to place the eggs) in their aquarium, even without the presence of a female. This behavior is generally considered a sign of well-being.

Depending on your betta's temperament, it may be possible to consider other peaceful inhabitants in your tank if this one is large enough (greater than 15 gallons / 60 liters) and has sufficient plants and hiding places. For instance, placing a male betta with certain species of fairly large and dull-colored shrimp (such as Amano / Japonica) or certain snails (like ramshorn or bladder snails) is possible. However, it's necessary to take some preliminary precautions by researching the specific needs of each species (acclimatization, food, etc.) and by introducing the betta last. Note that there is always a significant risk that the betta may harm or kill the other individuals in the tank.

Females and sorority

Female bettas are generally less aggressive than their male counterparts (although I have encountered some very aggressive females as well !). Naturally less ornate with duller colors and shorter fins, selective breeding has now produced some very beautiful female specimens as well.

The cohabitation of several females is possible by respecting certain rules :

- A generously planted aquarium to provide plenty of hiding places
- A minimum of 5 gallons (20 liters) per fish
- At least 3 individuals (with only 2 females, one would be submissive and constantly harassed by the other)

However, you must always be prepared to intervene in case of sudden aggression issues and have a backup aquarium ready to accommodate any mistreated female(s).

The ideal aquarium

Before even considering purchasing your betta, you must prepare the aquarium that will house it. This point is the most crucial because it will largely determine the quality of life and lifespan of your future fish. Indeed, a poorly prepared and unsuitable aquarium will drastically reduce its longevity.

Although the betta is relatively hardy by nature, it still has specific needs that must be met. We will examine in detail all the elements to include to achieve this in this section. But first, let's look at what not to do :

This image, found on the web, encapsulates all the mistakes and worst possible maintenance conditions for a betta fish. It serves as a perfect example of what not to do when keeping these beautiful creatures.

X Inadequate Tank Size (less than 6 gallons or 20 liters)

X Several male individuals housed together

X Lack of essential equipment (heating, filtration, natural decorations offering hiding places, etc.)

The ideal aquarium

Tank

As we have just seen, the aquarium must be of a suitable size for a betta. Certainly, it is possible to keep a betta in a very small space. The argument regularly put forward (especially by pet store sellers who are only looking to make a sale) is that in its natural state, the betta can live in a puddle. While this is not entirely false, it must be understood that this context only occurs during a limited period of the year (dry season) and does not represent the ideal living condition for the fish, but rather one of the environments to which it has adapted for survival.

To make an analogy, you and I are totally capable of surviving in a 12 sq yd (10 sq m) apartment. However, we would be much more comfortable in a 35 or even 70 sq yd (29 or 59 sq m) space (and even more so if we have to live confined there). The same logic must then be applied to your fish (and indeed, in general, to almost any animal kept in captivity) : The bigger, the better !

A larger space will allow your fish to fully develop by swimming and exploring its environment in depth, to the delight of your eyes.

We should then forget the standard containers :

- Jar or bowl (suitable for no animal life)
- "Betta box" (too small)
- Vase or any other similar type of container

Instead, we prefer :

- Square or rectangular tank of at least 5 gallons (19 liters). 3 gallons (11 liters) is the strict minimum.
- Tank that is longer/wider than it is high. As bettas are fish that need to regularly come to the surface to breathe, they will appreciate a modest depth of water (8 inches / 20 cm maximum, not including the thickness of the substrate).

Remember, providing an appropriately sized aquarium is crucial for the health and well-being of your betta. It allows for better water quality maintenance, more stable water parameters, and gives your fish the space it needs to exhibit natural behaviors.

The ideal aquarium

Heater

After the size and shape of the aquarium, heating is the second non-negotiable criterion, especially if the temperature of the room that will house your fish is not high enough (< 75°F / 24°C). In its natural habitat, a betta lives in a warm environment, between 75 and 83°F (24-28°C). As with the volume of its aquarium and many other parameters, the betta can accommodate and survive at lower temperatures. However, once again, you should strive to offer it the best possible living conditions to avoid any stress and risk of illness. Too low temperature is one of the main risk factors for its health.

You will need to equip your tank with an immersion heater. To ensure you buy the most compatible model for your tank, several criteria must be taken into account:

-> **A thermostat** : Look for a heater with a thermostat, which will allow you to adjust the temperature precisely to a chosen value. It will be triggered each time the water temperature drops below this threshold value. There are also preset immersion heaters that maintain a temperature of 77°F (25°C), perfectly suited for bettas.

-> **The power** : On average, you need 4W for 1 gallon of water (about 1W per liter). For a 5-gallon (19-liter) aquarium, a 20W heater is typically sufficient. If the room where the aquarium will be located is below 57°F (14°C), count 8W per gallon (about 2W per liter). A higher power won't be problematic as long as the heater is equipped with a thermostat. However, be mindful of the dimensions, ensuring that it fits well in your aquarium. Higher power usually means larger heaters.

You will also need to equip your aquarium with a **thermometer** to check the correct water temperature. This is useful in case of equipment failure of the heating system or during high temperatures in summer...

Finally, concerning the location of the heater in the aquarium, ideally place the heater as close as possible to the filtration pump (if present). This ensures mixing of the heated water and homogeneous diffusion of heat throughout the tank.

The ideal aquarium

Filtration

Filtration is not vital for the fish but it is for the aquarium and its biological balance. In other words, it helps maintain a healthy and viable environment for your fish by relieving you of certain maintenance tasks. It is therefore strongly recommended.

Indeed, it allows to purify the water in different ways. Mechanically first, by sucking up and trapping the waste and particles present in suspension in the aquarium. Also in a biological way, by allowing the degradation of all the toxic chemical compounds (from organic waste) into other compounds less dangerous for aquatic life (what is called the nitrogen cycle, see section - Water - page 25). A third filtration, called chemical, can be used but only for specific needs (such as to eliminate drug residues after a treatment or to intervene on certain chemical parameters of the water for example).

To best ensure these different functions, your filtration must respect a few characteristics.

-> **Sufficient flow** : From 2 to 3 times the volume of your aquarium per hour. For a 5 gallon (19 liter) aquarium, a filter with a flow rate of around 15 gallon / hour (57 liter / hour) will be satisfactory.

-> **Suitable filter materials** : you may have already noticed that filters are often made up of "foams" and filter materials of different appearance and color. This does not meet an aesthetic criterion but a technical one. Some media are thus intended for mechanical filtration (white wadding or large-mesh foam blocks, generally blue), others intended for biological filtration (often solid and porous matter in the form of small gravel, beads or noodles such as pozzolan, ceramics, clay, etc). Finally, those allowing chemical purification are often blocks of black activated carbon media.

Your filter must be composed of elements allowing mechanical filtration on the one hand and elements allowing biological filtration on the other.

-> **An adjustable outflow** : bettas are not made to swim in strong current environments. It is then necessary that the water outlet on your filter is adjustable so as to have a very weak current or that it is directed on a wall of the aquarium to break the force of the jet. If the filter in your possession doesn't allow this, you can try plugging the outlet slightly with a small piece of filtering foam (wadding type). However, be sure to secure it correctly, for example by surrounding it with tights-type stockings for women, held in place by an elastic band.

Regarding the different types of filters that can be found on the market (internal, external, suspended in cascade, enhancer,...) most are suitable for bettas as long as they respect the previous criteria. It's up to you to define which one best meets the configuration and aesthetics you expect for your aquarium.

If you do not want to use a filter, it is quite possible to do without it but you will then have to be even more rigorous in the maintenance of your tank. Without filtration, the water naturally becomes soiled more quickly. It is then necessary to carry out much more frequent and important water changes. We will explain this procedure in detail in the section - Maintaining the aquarium - (page 41).

Filter types that can be used :

Internal filter	Waterfall filter	Enhancer filter

Internal filter
+ Silent
  Filtration volume
  Discreet
- Clutter a "useful" volume in tank
  Maintenance

Waterfall filter
+ Does not clutter the volume
  Maintenance
- Noisy (it is aptly named Cascade)
  Not discreet

Enhancer filter
+ Low current
  Suitable for small volumes
  Price
- Slightly noisy
  Unsightly
  Provide for the purchase of an air pump (rarely supplied)

Note : once installed in the aquarium, the filter should run continuously without being unplugged. It will be only during aquarium maintenance.

The ideal aquarium

Lighting 💡

Lighting in an aquarium provides two functions. First, it illuminates the aquarium allowing you to make the most of your contemplation. Secondly, it makes it possible to artificially recreate a diurnal, day/night cycle. Many biochemical and metabolic processes (and not only in fish but in all living things in general) depend on this cycle. If this is disturbed, it can create latent stress in living organisms, gradually opening the door to disease for your fish. If your aquarium is in a room with enough natural light, this will be sufficient in most cases for fish. However, natural plants (if you plant them) have greater and more demanding light requirements than fish and that natural room light will not be able to satisfy. It will then be necessary to turn to an artificial lighting system for them. To be suitable, the lighting must also meet certain criteria.

-> **The type** : today we mainly find LED lighting on the market. They have the advantage of consuming less electricity, heating less and having a longer lifespan than conventional neon tubes, in addition to being more stylish.

-> **The power (in W) for neon tubes or the quantity of light (in Lumen) for LEDs** : it depends solely on the level of vegetation desired in your aquarium. 0.5W or 25 Lumens per liter of water (~2W or 100 Lumens / gallon) is a good average. For a very planted tank, it will take more with ~ 1W or 40 Lumens / liter (~ 4W or 160 Lumens / gallon).

Regardless of the lighting system, it will be connected to a timer which will automate the switching on of the light at a fixed time. <u>The cycles must be continuous.</u>

▲ In addition to its biological function, the lighting will highlight your betta and the decor of its aquarium so that you can observe them at best !

The ideal aquarium

The water

Water is the major and most important element of your aquarium. Its chemical composition and quality must be perfect if you want to keep your betta healthy. As seen, its quality depends on effective mechanical and biological filtration. However, there are a number of chemical parameters, dependent but also independent of filtration, to be checked regularly.

To ensure that you have good values, it is imperative that you carry out tests on your water, in particular for the chemical quantities presented below.

pH (degrees of acidity)

pH measures the acidity level of a liquid. It ranges from 0 to 14 and the more its value tends towards 0, the more we speak of an acidic medium. For example, sodas have a pH of around 3. On the contrary, the more the pH value tends towards 14, the more we will speak of an alkaline (or basic) environment. Between these two extreme values, i.e. around ~7, the pH will be qualified as neutral.

In general, in aquariums, a neutral or even slightly acidic pH will be the most suitable for most fish, including our bettas. But beyond the value (as long as it is within a reasonable range between 6 and 8) it is the sudden variations that will be the most dangerous (valid for the pH but also for any other parameter such as temperature).

0	6	7	14
Acid environment	*Optimal range*	*Basic or alkaline environment*	

The tests

You can do your own water testing by buying your own kits, but these are often expensive. The alternative may be to take a sample of your aquarium water to a pet store to do the test for you. Most agree to do this for free. Unfortunately, they are often carried out using strips, containing reagents and on which a drop of water from the aquarium is deposited. The disadvantage of this type of test is that they are imprecise or even totally incorrect. It is rather necessary to turn to tests in the form of drops to be poured into a precise quantity of water of the aquarium and whose change of color will precisely inform the desired value.

GH measures the mineral content of water. Depending on the concentrations of the various minerals present, the water will be more or less soft or very hard. It is this phenomenon in particular that explains why, depending the region and the origin of the water, more or less soap will be needed to obtain foam when washing your hands, for example. A small amount of soap will be sufficient with soft water, while a much larger amount will be needed with hard water.

A GH between 7 and 20° is to be maintained for most fish, including bettas.

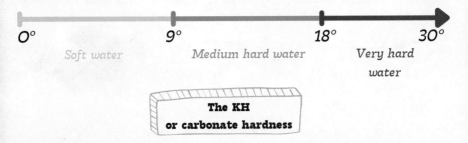

| 0° | 9° | 18° | 30° |
| Soft water | Medium hard water | Very hard water | |

The KH
or carbonate hardness

The KH is a component of the GH which only measures the level of carbonate in the water (more precisely the hydrogen carbonate ions also called bicarbonates). This quantity is crucial in the aquarium since it plays a direct role on the pH by preventing or attenuating its variations: this is what is called the buffering capacity (= capacity to dissolve a quantity of acids or bases). The higher the KH, the greater the buffering power of the water and the more difficult the pH will be to modify. This is why before being able to modify the pH of water, it is necessary to lower its KH, i.e. the resistance of water to variations in pH.

Be careful, in the event of insufficient CO_2 in the water, the plants will draw the necessary carbon from the hydrogen carbonate ions, which can dangerously lower the KH... This phenomenon is called "biogenic decalcification". It is recognized in particular by the presence of white spots on the plastics of the filter or the suction cups and then on the leaves of the plants when the condition becomes critical. There follows a sudden increase in pH which can be fatal to the aquarium and its inhabitants.

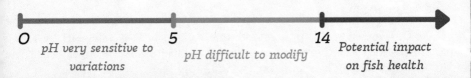

| 0 | 5 | 14 |
| pH very sensitive to variations | pH difficult to modify | Potential impact on fish health |

CO2, KH and PH

   The biogenic decalcification mentioned above highlights the existing interaction between CO2, KH and pH. We observe that when the CO2 content varies (here decrease linked to absorption by the plants) we also directly vary the KH (downward) and the pH (upward). This is due to the fact that the pH mainly results from the combination between KH and CO2.
When there is not enough carbon provided by CO2 for plants, they use a secondary source: hydrogen carbonate ions. By being absorbed, these decrease (the KH) and therefore naturally lower the buffering capacity of water which in turn allows significant variations in pH.

There are thus optimal values between pH and KH to respect for a perfect balance. For example, having a pH of 6.3 with a KH of 4 would not be suitable in most cases, because the concentration of CO2 present would be too high for the life of the fish. The value of the KH is always to be interpreted according to that of the pH.

The optimal PH parameters that can be obtained as a function of KH are :

KH	PH
1	[6.1 and 6.6]
2	[6.3 and 6.7]
3	[6.5 and 6.9]
4	[6.6 and 7.1]
5	[6.7 and 7.2]
6	[6.8 and 7.3]
7	[6.9 and 7.3]

If with your KH you have pH values lower than those given above, it means that there is too much CO2 in the water. On the contrary, if you have pH values higher than those given above, it means that there is too much O2 and not enough CO2.

Once this correlation is understood, one can easily vary one's pH by first adjusting one's KH (by replacing a part of aquarium water with water at the lower KH) and then by regulating the CO2 supply.

Ammonium (NH4), Nitrite (NO2) et Nitrate (NO3)

This trio of molecules composed of nitrogen (N) together form the nitrogen cycle. This phenomenon is one of the most important to know and respect in aquariums. If you've studied a bit of chemistry in your life, you must have heard the famous quote from chemist Antoine Lavoisier:

"Nothing is lost, nothing is created, everything is transformed".

The nitrogen cycle is a principle in aquariums that is based word for word on this quote. It represents the process of degradation of various organic waste (fish excrement, food scraps, plant residues, etc.) which are successively transformed into various chemical substances under the action of bacteria. First in ammonia, highly toxic, then in nitrites also very toxic at low concentrations and finally in less toxic nitrates which will in turn be consumed by the vegetation. This cycle represents the biological filtration of the aquarium and requires the presence of good bacteria. However, these bacteria need a certain amount of time and appropriate supports to develop. Hence the presence of the filter media mentioned in the filtration section such as pozzolan, ceramic noodles or any type of porous material that promotes the attachment of bacteria. Your aquarium soil will also be a great reservoir of these good bacteria.
You must wait at least 3 weeks when putting a new tank in water before adding the fish, so that the bacteria can first colonize the aquarium and install this cycle !

Optimal and maximum tolerable values for each substance :

Ammonia (NH4) : 0 ppm and 0 ppm, if ammonia is present in your tank it means that it has either not been cycled or that a deep imbalance has taken place killing the good bacteria.

-> You have to start the cycling process again by removing the fish or changing 50% of the water every 2 days and leaving the filtration running.

Nitrites (NO2) : 0 ppm and 0,2 ppm, if the level of nitrites exceeds 0.2 ppm they can become fatal for fish. A water change of at least 30% every 2 days is recommended until the rate drops below 0.2 ppm.

Nitrates (NO3) : Up to 25 ppm and 50 ppm. Nitrates are necessary for the plants that feed on them. However, past a certain rate, it is the algae that benefit, promoting their proliferation.

-> From 50 ppm, a water change of at least 30% should be carried out.

Osmosis water

Osmosis water is pure water, filtered to remove all minerals and retain only water molecules (H_2O). In general, to act on the main parameters of the water, it will be necessary to use reverse osmosis water, to be diluted with another mineralized water (bottle or tap) or by remineralizing oneself with mineral salts. By varying the proportion of each, it is thus possible to obtain the desired parameters in the most precise manner.

Unless your running water has parameters that are really unsuitable for the fighter's needs (which is still possible depending on your region), it is unlikely that you will need reverse osmosis water.

Oxygen (O2) and CO2

In the case of a betta fish aquarium, these two quantities are of little importance since it recovers all the oxygen it needs by sucking the air directly from the surface of the aquarium. If the tank has significant vegetation, a CO_2 injection system may be useful to ensure optimal plant growth (as well as if you wish to plant plants with reddened leaves, only possible with powerful lighting and a significant amount of CO_2). There are many possibilities for the implementation of such a system, which can be purchased directly from shops or can even be manufactured by oneself (tutorial available on the internet by searching for "DIY CO2"). It is nevertheless necessary to make sure before embarking on this project that you have understood the different chemical interactions taking place in the water and to size the system as well as possible in order to have the adequate quantity of CO_2.

ℹ **Water problem**
Faced with a major water problem, the first reflex to adopt is to react quickly by replacing a large quantity of water in the aquarium with new, healthy water. The second step is to determine what may be the cause of the problem in order to avoid a recurrence (population level adapted to the size of the tank, cycling of the aquarium, regular maintenance, etc.) A cause that is often overlooked and yet frequent is the analysis of new water used for water changes. If it is running tap water, it may be that your settings problems could come from there..!

The ideal aquarium

The decoration

The decoration of your tank depends only on you and your tastes. It will still be important for your fighter to provide him with a safe environment with hiding places that he can use for example. But also important for the benefits it can bring to your tank. Let's take a look at the different decorative elements that can make up an aquarium.

Plants

Please, go for natural plants! I hate (and I weigh my words) artificial plants, fabric or plastic. They only have flaws for me and have no place in an aquarium supposed to reconstitute a piece of nature. Certainly natural plants are more demanding and require (a little) more effort in terms of maintenance, but this is nothing in return for the benefits they bring :

- biologically balance the water (consume nitrates, CO_2 and oxygenate the water)
- slow down the development of algae by competing with them (both consume the same nutrients)
- are safe for your fish (plastic plants can be sharp on their edges and damage the fins of the betta)
- are much more aesthetic (this point is purely subjective and engages only me, but all the same...)

Need of plants

Good quality and sufficient quantity of light is essential (see section - Lighting - page 21). It will be necessary to light little the first weeks (~7h per day) to gradually reach 10 to 12h of lighting per day (30 minutes to 1h of additional lighting per week from the second week is a good compromise according to my experience).

Provide all the necessary nutrients (iron, copper, potassium, calcium, etc.) using a suitable substrate placed under the soil, technical soil or via the supply of regular fertilizers (in ball or liquid form).

Install a CO_2 injection system (mandatory if you are like me, lover of tanks with natural and luxuriant vegetation !).

Choice of plants

Then comes the choice of plants. Unfortunately, it will have to be done according to the characteristics of your aquarium seen previously and not only your tastes. It must also take into account the characteristics of the plants themselves: growth rate, size, etc. All this may seem complicated but don't worry, we will see together the plants that will best match if you are just starting out, namely plants that are not very demanding.

If your aquarium is equipped with the bare minimum (low lighting, no nutrient soil, no CO2, etc.) or if you have not yet mastered all the notions of aquariums, you will have to turn to so-called "easy" plants. It will also be necessary among these to make a mix between fast-growing plants (to limit the parallel development of algae) and slow-growing plants (so as not to deplete all nutrients such as CO2).

Below is a small list that you can use to make your choice.

Slow growing plants :

- Cryptocorynes (e.g. wendtii, parva or affinis species)
- Java fern (microsorum pteropus)
- Java moss (vesicularia dubayana)
- The dwarf anubias (anubia nana)

Fast growing plants :

- Echinodorus (Bleher)
- Hygrophilas (polysperma, corymbosa, difformis)
- Bolbitis of Heudelot (bolbitis heudelotii)
- Waterweed, (Egeria densa)

You can put four to five different plants in a 5 gallon (obviously more in a larger liter).

 Plants with rhizomes
Some plants have rhizomes, this is particularly the case of anubias and java fern. For this type of epiphytic plants, it is not necessary to bury the rhizome (the root) in the substrate but to attach it (using nylon thread, fishing line, sewing thread or aquarium-safe glue) to a root or a stone.

Maintenance

To live and have normal growth, plants have specific needs: an adequate temperature, a sufficient supply of light, water with the appropriate parameters (pH, KH, GH, CO2) and nutrients in the right quantity, neither too much nor too little (Nitrate, Phosphate, Potassium, Iron, Copper, etc.)
In particular, there are two types of deficiency, which can explain the growth retardation or the death of a plant :

- Deficiency due to the absence of a necessary nutrient, which is the easiest to remedy with appropriate fertilization.

- Induced deficiency, due to an impossible assimilation of a type of nutrient by the plant. This happens in the case of an unbalanced pH (outside the range 6 - 7) or an imbalance linked to the quantity of elements present (example: too many nitrates, too much light, not enough iron, potassium, etc.).

Nutrients are mainly provided by water. But a supplement by using technical soil or adding a nutrient substrate under the gravel or by adding liquid fertilizer directly to the water can be beneficial or even essential for certain demanding plants ! The table on the following page can help you identify certain cause(s) of deficiency according to the symptoms observed on your plants.

Beyond these elements, maintenance will boil down to pruning the plants when the need arises: cutting damaged leaves, those covered with algae or which have become too invasive.

▲ Tank with lush vegetation not lacking in any nutrients !

Table listing some problems that can arise on your plants and their potential causes.

	Slow growing	weak plants	Holes in leaves	Whole yellow leaves	Yellow between the veins	Yellow leaf edges	reddened leaves	Distorted leaves	Rolled up leaves	blistered leaves	Brown/black leaves	leaf blight	Leaves that "melt"	Leaf detachment	On young leaves	On old leaves	On all the leaves	Abnormal knot distance	Root necrosis
Temperature too low	X																		
Temperature too high					X												X		
Lack of maintenance			X										X				X		
Lack of light		X	X																
Excess light						X					X								
Unsuitable light spectrum																	X		
CO2 deficiency	X																		
Excess Nitrate								X								X			
Excess Phosphate										X									
Bad planting				X							X			X					
Iron deficiency					X										X				
Potassium deficiency		X						X											
Phosphate deficiency				X												X			
Nitrogen deficiency	X			X															
Manganese deficiency					X									X					
Calcium deficiency						X									X				
Magnesium deficiency					X											X			
Sodium deficiency	X																		
Boron deficiency								X											X
Molybdenum deficiency					X														
Copper deficiency						X	X												
Zinc deficiency		X			X														
Snails / Fish / Insects			X														X		

The floor

As we have seen, the soil of the floor plays a decorative but also useful role by providing support for good bacteria and a nutrient supply for plants. Several choices of soil are available to you:

- A technical / complete soil : it is used alone and allows to have ideal water parameters for the bettas with the use of reverse osmosis water. It also provides good quality nutrients for plants.

- Soil made up of a nutritious substrate and covered with neutral soil such as sand or gravel. You can choose the ground according to your tastes as long as it is not abrasive for the bettas (avoid quartz gravels with too large a grain size for example).

Stones, roots and other elements

These elements are intended to provide hiding places for your fighter and to make your tank aesthetic. Their choices depend only on your tastes but to avoid certain disappointments, some good reflexes are necessary all the same.

Roots can be purchased or collected from the wild. In both cases (but particularly the second) it will be necessary to make sure not to introduce harmful elements (molds, fungi, bacteria, parasites, ...) in your aquarium, which can accompany your roots. Soaking in boiling water for one to two hours will eliminate any potential hazard. In addition, this operation will make it possible to saturate the roots with water in order to make them sink more easily (if this is not enough, weigh them down with a stone for example, until they no longer float). Note that it is normal to observe the development of white mold on them during the first weeks.

The stones, just like the roots, can be bought or picked up. It will nevertheless be necessary to inquire about their type (limestone to be avoided, granite, slate, schist, volcanic, ...) The stones that one picks up oneself must be rubbed, scraped and ideally boiled to get rid of potential unwanted hosts.

The other elements can be diverse and varied (as long as they do not pollute or modify the parameters of the water). Natural is best, as the half-coconuts offer good hiding places for our fighters. You can also place half terracotta flower pots covered with java moss or buy ready-made decorations if you like that. Prefer decorations in resin and not in plastic.

<u>Central point</u> : always make sure that the elements introduced will not be dangerous for your fish, with the risk of cuts in particular (you can do the "pantyhose test", which consists of rubbing a pair of tights against the element to be checked - if it snags or tears, the same will happen to your fighter's fins and should therefore be avoided).

The catappa leaf from the Indian Almond tree (Terminalia catappa) is a very interesting element to use in aquariums and particularly with bettas. These leaves, in dried form, have antifungal, antioxidant and antibacterial properties in addition to coloring the water with a reassuring amber color for the fish.

▲ Catappa leaves are easily found in pet stores or on internet.

The ideal aquarium

Installation

Below is a table summarizing the equipment to be provided according to the size of your tank :

Dimensions (inch)	Volume (gallon)	Tank weight (kg)	Minimum lighting	Heating (W)	Filter flow rate	Floor (with substrate)	Total weight
10 x 14 x 12	5	3	10W or 500 Lumens	25W	15 g/hour	6 kg	28kg
12 x 12 x 14	8	5	15W or 750 Lumens	50W	25 g/hour	9 kg	39kg
20 x 10 x 12	10	6	20W or 1000 Lumens	50W	30 g/hour	12 kg	52kg

A completely filled aquarium weighs a considerable amount. Make sure you place it on a piece of furniture that can support it, perfectly level and in a suitable location so that you don't have to move it later. Similarly, always place a flexible element between the aquarium and the support (such as a carpet, yoga mat or expanded polystyrene at least 2cm thick) which will absorb any irregularities of the support and prevent the aquarium from breaking under its own weight. Supports to be placed under the four corners of the aquarium are also possible.

An ideal location is in any room of the house except the kitchen and the bathroom (vapors, grease and cosmetic products are harmful). You should also avoid placing the aquarium in direct sunlight, which would encourage the proliferation of green algae and could dangerously raise the temperature in summer.

Preparation and welcoming

Aquarium launching

You now have all the knowledge you need to welcome and maintain your future little fish in the best possible conditions. Now on to practice !

The first step after buying all the equipment (but especially not the fish, patience!) will be to put everything in place. Steps for this:

1 Start by rinsing your bare tank. Place it on its support and don't forget to place a flexible element underneath.
If you have opted for a nutrient substrate for your plants, put it before the real soil without rinsing it, until it is about 1 inch (3 cm) thick.

For aesthetic reasons, make a groove on the visible sides of the aquarium so that you cannot distinguish the different layers of substrate (the real soil will fill in the groove and you will only see it through the glass).

2 Then put your soil after having rinsed it thoroughly in a bucket of water, to an average thickness of about 2 inch or 5 cm (to be adjusted according to the height of your aquarium).

The ideal is to spread it in a gentle slope, putting a larger layer in the back than on the front. This will accentuate the effect of depth in the aquarium and give it a more voluminous appearance.

3 Place the filtration, the heating and the various decorative elements such as roots and stones in order to have a rendering that you like

In order to keep a certain visual harmony, it is preferable to use stones and wood of the same type (if several roots and several stones). The largest elements will be placed at the back in order to accentuate this notion of depth even more.

4 Plant your different plants in small bunches after having rinsed them well with clear water. If you buy them commercially, they are often kept in several stems in pots surrounded by rock wool. This wool must be removed as much as possible without damaging the roots.

5 Fill your aquarium with water with the appropriate parameters. In order not to upset the whole decor, place a plate at the bottom or your hand, on which you will run the water in order to "break" the water jet.

6 Finally power up all equipment (pump, heating, lighting)

Preparation and welcoming

Cycle start

Here is your tank in place and all your equipment is working properly. It is now necessary to start the nitrogen cycle (review part - water -). In reality, the cycle starts by itself as soon as the tank is filled with water, with the first waste produced by the plants. But to further initiate this first step which consists in developing the first bacteria transforming ammonia into nitrites, you can add a light pinch of food to the water.

A technique of artificially seeding the aquarium is also possible. It consists of manually introducing these famous "good bacteria" into the aquarium, via two different methods :

1. You can either recover part of the filter media from a healthy and already cycled tank to put them in your own filtration. In this way, the bacteria from the other aquarium will colonize your tank and its filtration more quickly.

2. You can also buy ready-to-use bacteria vials directly from the shops.
   I am personally not a fan of this method, it does not offer any guarantee on the quality and effectiveness of the bacteria, which vary according to the brands used.

These two methods can speed up the cycle for the most impatient, but it is also just as possible (and recommended) to let nature take its course and wait three to four weeks for the bacteria to naturally colonize your aquarium.

Regardless of the method chosen, one step will remain essential: regularly check the parameters of your water and particularly the level of nitrites. It is this value that will give the green light for the introduction of your fighter, when it has gone through a higher level and then has come down to 0 ppm.

Nitrogen cycle in the aquarium : under the effect of various bacteria, the waste is transformed into NH4, the NH4 is degraded into NO2 then the NO2 into NO3. NO3 is then consumed by plants (and algae).

Preparation and welcoming

Choose your betta

It's good ! Your tank is finally cycled, the nitrites have gone through a peak before falling back to 0 ppm and life has already developed in your little aquatic world (plants have grown and small harmless beings like snails have invited themselves !). It's finally time to pick up your long-awaited betta !

For this, several choices are available to you. You can go to a pet store, directly to a passionate breeder if there is one near you or even order it on the internet... But in order to avoid any disappointment, it is advisable to move to be able to observe and choose your betta as well as possible. If the aesthetics of the latter will play a major role in your choice, it is absolutely necessary that you take the time to look carefully at the appearance and behavior of the future chosen one. These elements testify to his general good health, so be careful !

A positive behavior translates into active swimming (insofar as the aquarium where it is located allows it without constraint, too strong a filtration for example will tend to immobilize the fish in a calm corner). He should also be responsive and inquisitive (you can place your finger on the wall without tapping, which should make him react). For some, it is even possible to make them parade (swollen gills and deployed fins) by presenting them to their reflection thanks to a small mirror.
On the contrary, a betta with poor health will be amorphous, lying on the bottom of the aquarium without reactions.

▲ A betta in good health

In appearance, a betta fish in good health must have smooth scales, whole fins (neither damaged nor torn), with more or less bright colors. Torn or bristly scales, white dots, white "cotton" on the body or head or torn fins indicate a poor state of health.

A betta that's responsive, curious, lively, and displays its body and fins in perfect condition when you show it its reflection in a mirror or in front of another betta, is sure to be the right choice !

 Good to know
In some pet stores, although bettas are in separate tanks, it may be that the filtration (if there is one) is common to all with the same water circulating in all the aquariums. In this case, a sick fish could infect all the others. It is better then to avoid buying one of these fish, even of healthy appearance (disease being able to declare itself later).

Preparation and welcoming

Acclimatization

Once your fish has been chosen, try not to delay bringing it home to limit the stress caused. Upon arrival, the first thing not to do is to transfer your betta directly with the water from his bag into his new aquarium. Not knowing the quality of the water where your fish comes from, it is safer to throw it away to avoid any contamination of your tank.

Similarly, the parameters and the temperature of the two waters being undoubtedly very different, it will be necessary to proceed with a gradual acclimatization. To do this, follow these steps :

Step 1

Place the bag containing your fish directly in your aquarium so that it floats there. Open it up and make sure you secure it properly (with a clamp or the lid) so it doesn't leak and the fish can't jump out. This will allow the temperatures of the two waters to gradually balance. Turn off the lighting of your aquarium and limit the light in the room where it is located as much as possible. Fish are very sensitive to light and keeping them in the dark helps to reduce stress level.

Step 2

After about 10/15 minutes, take about half a glass of water from your aquarium and pour it gently into the fish bag. Repeat this operation every ten minutes for about 1 hour.

Step 3

When you've added as much aquarium water as there was originally in the bag (approximately) it's time to release your fish into their new home. You can catch it using a small landing net or ideally by hand to avoid any injury. Just be sure to wash your hands thoroughly before or wear surgical gloves to avoid contamination.

Turn off the light and then let the fish rest overnight.

Care and maintenance

Food

The betta is a carnivorous predator that feeds in the wild on small live prey. It is therefore necessary to ensure that it provides enough protein through its diet.

There are different solutions for this. Some are more suitable than others, but the main thing is to diversify the type of food as much as possible.

Dry Food

This is the most well-known type of food. Dry food, such as flakes or pellets, is to be used as a staple food for fighters. However, not all products available on the market are equal from a quality point of view. To be sure of making the right choice, refer to the packaging and check the composition of the product : it must contain at least 30% protein. If this is not the case, this means that most of the ingredients are other than animal products (often cereal flours) and therefore not very suitable and balanced for the carnivorous diet of the betta.

Depending on the betta and their more or less capricious character, it is common for some to refuse flakes (and more rarely granules). In this case, it is necessary to offer them over several days so that they get used to this form of food. In most cases, the pellets end up being well accepted.

▲ Example of pellets containing 41% protein and accepted by most fish

Why avoid flakes ?

Flakes are generally not recommended because, in addition to being frequently shunned, they have the defect of swelling on contact with water and inside the stomach of the fish which can cause digestion problems depending on the individual. However you can do a compatibility test with your fish

Care and maintenance

Food

Food alive

Live food, consisting of small insects or crustaceans (mosquito larvae, brine shrimp, daphnia, bloodworms, etc.) is the preferred type of food for fighting fish. It stimulates their hunting instinct and perfectly covers their nutritional needs. Live food can be obtained from pet stores in the form of plates comprising several small cubes of water. It is also possible to do your own breeding in a small dedicated tank (many tutorials exist on the internet, especially on the breeding of brine shrimp). Finally, some insects can be collected directly from the wild (especially mosquito larvae in summer). It is just necessary to check that the place of collection is not polluted and to rinse the insects before any introduction into the aquarium (with a small landing net for example). You can even give guppy-type fish fry if you or someone you know has them, which also helps to regulate the extreme proliferation of this species !

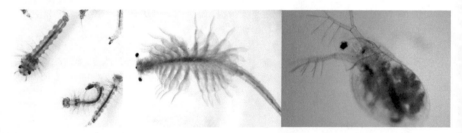

▲ Food of choice for your betta with in order : mosquito larvae, brine shrimp and daphnia... Yum !

Frozen or freeze-dried

The live prey presented above can also be purchased from pet stores in the form of frozen or freeze-dried cubes. This alternative allows for much longer storage, unlike live food which, once opened, must be consumed after a few days at most. This form of food is therefore more interesting if you only have one fighter, as the cubes can be cut easily.

ℹ **Live food**
Although nutritionally richer and more stimulating for your betta, live food should not make up your fish's main diet. Worms (bloodworms, tubifex, etc.) in particular should be given occasionally to avoid any digestive problems.

Care and maintenance

Food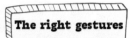

The right gestures

Betta is a very greedy fish. As long as you serve him the meal, he will come to the table ! It is therefore necessary to adopt the right gestures in the face of this behavior.

First, keep in mind that the betta's stomach is barely bigger than his eye. About three bites are enough to fill it up and this should be the optimal amount to give in one meal, twice a day. If you cannot organize the feeding in two meals, then it will be necessary to give at most six mouthfuls during a single meal per day (for example six pellets). Meal time doesn't matter.

Besides not having a big stomach, betta fish don't have a digestive system meant to work full time. It is therefore wise to put them on a diet one day a week. Remember that with bettas, it is better to feed too little than too much !

Finally, it is recommended to vary the type of food as much as possible over the course of a week, avoiding giving the same food on two consecutive days (see example below).

Mealtime is the time to watch your fish carefully. If it refuses to eat, this may reflect unsuitable food (insist on several days or switch to another type) or more serious, a health problem. Uneaten food should be promptly removed from the aquarium to avoid excessive pollution.

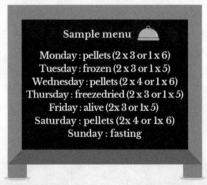

Sample menu

Monday : pellets (2 x 3 or 1 x 6)
Tuesday : frozen (2 x 3 or 1 x 5)
Wednesday : pellets (2 x 4 or 1 x 6)
Thursday : freezedried (2 x 3 or 1 x 5)
Friday : alive (2x 3 or 1x 5)
Saturday : pellets (2x 4 or 1x 6)
Sunday : fasting

 Helpful hints
Some brands market under the same product several types of food such as granules, flakes, brine shrimp and crisps. These 4-in-1 menus can, together with an additional source of live food, be very practical for diversifying meals at a lower cost.

Care and maintenance

Maintain the aquarium

Depending on the size, equipment and layout of your aquarium, maintenance will not be quite the same, especially in terms of the frequency of water changes between a filtered and unfiltered aquarium. In any case, it is vital to keep your Betta's aquarium clean in order to ensure its well-being.

Cleaning

For the cleaning of any element (decorations, windows, filter,...) never use soap or any other household product which could seriously poison your aquarium and your fish. Aquarium water should be used as the only cleaner whenever possible. Similarly, try to intervene only on the bare minimum so as not to stress your betta too much. Everything that is decorative elements, stones, roots, etc., should therefore only be moved if they require deep cleaning outside the aquarium.

The decoration

If the decorations are dirty (in particular covered significantly by algae), remove them if necessary from the tank and scrub them under warm running water using a dedicated toothbrush. If you have natural plants in the same case, lightly rub the leaves little affected by the algae between your fingers in order to extract the maximum. Cut off completely rotten leaves.

The glasses

Recalcitrant white traces can form on the glass of your aquarium: limestone. As with the limestone in your bathroom, it is possible to apply white vinegar to a cloth and rub with it. The stains should come out without difficulty. Then wipe with a dry cloth and be careful not to spill vinegar into the aquarium water.

i The algae
All aquariums have algae in greater or lesser quantities. They are part of the ecosystem. Despite this, in the event of an invasion, it will be necessary to identify the type of algae present in order to find the cause. Filamentous green algae are for example often due to an excess of light/nitrates. Brown algae (diatoms) are due either to a young tank that is not yet balanced or to a high level of silica.

Care and maintenance

Maintain the aquarium

Water changes without filtration

As mentioned in the section - The ideal aquarium -, it is not mandatory to equip your aquarium with a filter. It is then necessary in this case to carry out water changes of 10/15% every two/three days in order to avoid the rise of a peak of nitrites.

For a 4 gallons aquarium, this will represent ~ 0.5 gallon of water to be replaced every three days.

For a 7 gallons aquarium, ~ 1 gallon every three days.

Before any water change, it will be necessary to ensure that the new water has approximately the same parameters as the water in the aquarium and that it is especially chlorine-free if you use tap water.

To eliminate chlorine, you can use water conditioning products sold in pet stores, or let the water sit in an open container for 48 hours (the chlorine evaporates in the open air). It is not necessary to take your fish out of its aquarium for these water changes. The use of a small siphon will allow you to suck up the water and waste at the bottom of the aquarium at the same time without disturbing your fish (as long as you don't suck

▲ Siphoning technique for water changes

its fins !). You can buy one or use bubbler silicone tubing which works just fine if the length is sufficient.

▲ Example of an aquarium siphon

Care and maintenance

Maintain the aquarium

Water changes with filtration

If your aquarium is equipped with filtration, maintenance will be much less regular. We will move to a water change of 10% once a week only. The cleaning of the filter and its filter media will be done approximately once a month depending on its level of clogging.

 Filter cleaning

The filter materials of the filter must not be rinsed with tap water. The chlorine would kill all the vital bacteria they contain. There would then follow a new peak of nitrites fatal for your fish. The cleaning of the filter materials should be done at the same time as one of the weekly water changes. Thus, with the old water removed from the aquarium you can rinse the filter materials without any risk. The masses don't have to be like new when put back into the filter, just make sure the bulk of the trash is removed. You can then replace the filter in the aquarium and discard the dirty water (you can also use it to water your plants, which will appreciate this quality natural fertilizer!)

When the filter materials seem really worn and porous (generally after 2/3 months), it will be necessary to replace them. But here again, a rule to follow: never replace all the filter media at the same time. It is necessary to change the used foam blocks only by half, by cutting them in half and replacing only one of the two. In this way, the bacteria of the old foam will colonize the new one (we will then change the second half of foam the following week).

If you think you have made a mistake in the maintenance of the filter that could be detrimental to the survival of bacteria, you will have to react quickly by applying the same water changes as in the case of an unfiltered aquarium (previous page). This procedure should be carried out until it is sure that the tank is completely cycled again and that there is no longer any risk of the presence of nitrites (confirmed by tests).

Care and maintenance

Diseases

Bettas are by nature very hardy fish. However, they remain like any living organism, susceptible to disease. Because if the betta resists well, once the disease is in place it can evolve very quickly and lead to the death of your fish in the vast majority of cases.

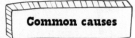

Common causes

Illnesses encountered with bettas often have the same causes. Knowing how to anticipate these causes in order to avoid the disease is the first step in the fight against it. And unsurprisingly, the most common cause is poor maintenance conditions :

- Unsuitable water parameters (pH, temperature, nitrites, etc.)
- Poor feeding (quality, diversity, overfeeding, etc.)
- Permanent stress (not enough hiding places, swimming volume too small, etc.)

These factors gradually weaken the immune system of the fish which is then no longer able to fight against external aggressions. The other cause is the introduction of a pathogenic agent into the aquarium (viruses, bacteria, fungi, etc). This is why it is essential to clean any element coming from outside (roots, stones, decoration, etc.) and to carry out a quarantine in an isolated tank for new plants and other living beings introduced.

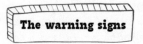

The warning signs

Any unusual change in behavior should alert you. The signs of a problem are however recurrent in the betta. Below is a non-exhaustive list of symptoms :

- Loss of appetite or spitting out food
- Difficult swimming, floating on the surface or in an upright position
- Amorphous, placed on a decorative element or at the bottom of the aquarium
- Physical abnormality (swollen belly, torn fins, white spots, ...)
- White stringy droppings sticking to the anus

It is important to be very attentive to the slightest symptom which will allow you to precisely identify the disease from which your fighter suffers and therefore to treat it as well as possible without risking to weaken the animal further. Now let's see a list of the main diseases found in the betta.

Care and maintenance

Diseases

White spots

Symptoms : Fins stuck to the body, disordered swimming, fish rubbing against the decorations. At the advanced stage of the disease only, presence of white spots of about 0.5 mm on the body and fins.

Causes : White spots are caused by a parasite called Ichthyophthirius multifiliis. Very contagious, its development takes place in two phases : the free phase where it reproduces outside the fish. And the infection phase where it colonizes its host.

Curability : White spots disease is generally treatable if you react quickly enough.

Treatment : Several treatments are possible

1st method : Treatment with antibacterial
To be carried out ideally in a hospital tank. Possible in the aquarium, but it will be necessary to provide filtration on activated carbon to eliminate drug residues and recycle the aquarium (antibacterial kill all bacteria, even the good ones!)

- Heat the tank above 84°F
- Use an antibacterial and follow the instructions

2nd method : treatment with salt (high concentration)
To be carried out in a hospital tank, invertebrates and plants do not tolerate salt. A high salt concentration will cause a sudden change in osmotic pressure. The cells of the fish are resistant to this shock but not those of the parasite. At high salt concentrations, it is very important to gradually desalinate the water (over several hours) and to use non-iodized and non-fluoridated salt.

- In a hospital tank heated above 84°F, add 100 grams of salt per gallon of water
- Then put the fish in it (after having acclimatized it to the temperature by placing it beforehand in a container floating on the surface of the hospital tank)
- Leave it for 15 minutes and desalinate gradually : replace 1/3 of the water with new water. Then 50% after one to two hours. Finally, another 50% an hour later.

In case of abnormal behavior during the bath (hazardous swimming, fish on the back, ...), it will be imperative to desalinate immediately and remove the betta.

Care and maintenance

Diseases

Dropsy

Symptoms : Swelling of the abdomen, loss of appetite, bulging eyes, mucous excrement in the form of milky white filaments, spiky scales giving the appearance of a "pine cone".

Causes : Dropsy is not a disease strictly speaking but a general weakening of the fish leading to different complications. It can be caused by several factors, independent or cumulative : poor maintenance, viral or bacterial infection, intense stress, unsuitable food ...

The intestine is often the first organ infected. The intestinal mucosa breaks down and is expelled in excrement in the form of white filaments. It becomes permeable, thus leaving an open field to the entry of pathogenic agents causing a cascade of other complications such as necrosis of the liver or kidneys and in turn causing renal failure. In the final stage, internal fluids that can no longer be eliminated accumulate in the abdominal cavities (swollen abdomen), in the pockets of the scales (ruffled skin) or behind the eyes (bulging eyes).

Curability : Dropsy is often fatal as symptoms become noticeable at an advanced stage of the disease.

Euthanasia is often the best possible end to consider, in order to avoid additional suffering for your fighter.

Treatment : A last chance treatment can be attempted, but its success rate remains relatively very low.

The procedure :

- Isolate the fish in a hospital tank with a capacity of 0,5 to 1 gallon
- Place only a small heater set between 88 and 90°F
    Many bacteria are much less active at these temperatures
- Dissolve a teaspoon of salt (~25g) per gallon of water (low concentration) and half a cattapa leaf
- Use a strong antibacterial and follow the instructions
- Place the tray in total darkness and apply the treatment for 3/4 days.

Fin Rot

 Symptoms : Torn fins, red lines (blood) may appear in the sails or on the tips of the fins when the disease is in an advanced state.

 Causes : Very common disease in the fighter due to his morphology. It can appear following an injury, a tear against an element of the decor for example. But also spontaneously, caused by significant stress, bacterial or viral infection or fungal infection.

 Curability : Depending on the progress of the rots, the treatment will be more or less easy. It is more complicated when the rot is on the dorsal fin or has reached the body.

 Treatment : is usually done with an antibacterial
To be carried out ideally in a hospital tank. Possible in the aquarium, but it will be necessary to provide filtration on activated carbon to eliminate drug residues and recycle the aquarium (antibacterial kill all bacteria, even the good ones !)

- Isolate the fish in a hospital tank with a capacity of 0,5 to 1 gallon
- Place only a small heater set at 75°F.
- Use an antibacterial and following the recommendations in the instructions

An osmotic bath with low concentration salt + cattapa is also possible at the start of the disease :

- Isolate the fish in a hospital tank with a capacity of 0,5 to 1 gallon
- Place only a small heater set between 75°F and 79°F.
- Dissolve a teaspoon of salt (~25g) per gallon of water and a cattapa leaf

Change the water every 1 to 2 days with water with the same parameters (temperature, salt concentration, etc.). The treatment is to be carried out until the regrowth of the fins (transparent parts at the end).

If the salt treatment proves ineffective after a few days and the rot worsens, quickly switch to a stronger antibacterial treatment.

Care and maintenance

Diceases

Symptoms : Dull and less supple sail and body colors (as if glued to glue), loss of appetite. Then white/yellowish spots appear on the skin and fins giving the impression that the fish has been coated in a golden powder. He rubs against the decor and the veils tighten. At an advanced stage of the disease, the skin of the fish literally shreds.

Causes : Oodinium is caused by a parasite clinging to and developing on the scales and gills of fish. Extremely contagious, it can be confused in the early stages with white spot disease.

Curability : More or less easily curable depending on the progress of the disease. Deadly if not treated in time.

Treatment : Several treatments are possible

1st method : treatment with antibacterial

To be carried out abso in a hospital tank. Possible in the aquarium, but it will be necessary to provide filtration on activated carbon to eliminate drug residues and recycle the aquarium (antibacterial kill all bacteria, even the good ones!)

- Place the hospital tank heated to 84°F in the dark

- Use an antibacterial and follow the instructions

2nd method : treatment with salt (high concentration)

Same procedure as for treating white spots (page 44)

A treatment of the entire tank should be considered to eradicate the parasites, before any reintroduction of fish into it.

Care and maintenance

Diseases

Constipation / indigestion

Symptoms : Swollen abdomen, loss of appetite, listlessness, little/no droppings or (dark colored) droppings that stick.

Causes : Unsuitable diet, too fatty (too many bloodworms for example), not diversified enough or overeating.

Curability : If simple constipation, the problem is usually resolved within a few days. Otherwise, look for another path of potentially more serious illness.

Treatment : Fasting for a few days (3-4 days). Giving her transit-promoting foods like blanched peas or pellets soaked in castor oil can help.
Parading it can promote the activation of transit.

An osmotic bath is also possible (Same procedure as for the treatment of fin rot page 46)

Once recovered, slowly resume feeding, following the instructions given in the - Feeding - part of this chapter.

Mycos - Fungus

Symptoms : Loss of appetite, discoloration, apathy, presence of cottony white patches on the body and head with long filaments (not to be confused with a bacterial infection such as Flexibacter columnaris, which also presents a cottony appearance without long filaments).

Causes : Poor maintenance with in particular too low a temperature which promotes the attack of fungus spores.

Curability : Easily curable, but should not be delayed in treatment.

Treatment : Performed with antifungal products in a hospital tank heated between 77 and 81°F.

Care and maintenance

Reproduction ⚥

One of the most intriguing aspects of Betta splendens care is their unique reproductive process. Reproducing bettas requires careful planning and specific steps to ensure the successful breeding of these stunning fish. In this part, we will explore the key stages and considerations involved in the reproduction of betta, shedding light on the intricacies of this particular process. From adult conditioning to tank setup and the delicate mating rituals, each step plays a crucial role in the successful propagation of these magnificent fish. Understanding the intricacies of betta reproduction will deepen your appreciation for these remarkable creatures and may even inspire you to embark on your own breeding journey.

Adult conditioning

Conditioning the adult is a foundational step in the intricate and captivating process of breeding. It is a phase that demands meticulous care, patience, and attention to detail, as it lays the essential groundwork for a successful breeding endeavor. This preparatory stage typically commences approximately one to three weeks before the actual reproduction is desired. During this critical period, focus on nurturing and enhancing the physical and physiological well-being of both the chosen male and female Bettas. The primary goal is to optimize their overall health and vitality to ensure a successful breeding experience.

A key aspect of conditioning revolves around the dietary regimen. To promote the ideal breeding condition, you need to increase the quantity and quality of food provided to the Betta pair. Live or frozen foods, such as freshly hatched artemias (brine shrimp) and nutrient-rich larvae, are preferred choices. These high-protein, live offerings provide essential nutrients and energy that are vital for both male and female Bettas as they prepare for the demanding reproductive activities ahead.

Interestingly, while the male Betta may not display any overt or dramatic physical changes during this conditioning phase, it is crucial to ensure that he accumulates sufficient reserves to withstand a brief period of fasting, which is an integral part of the Betta reproduction protocol. This fasting phase helps prepare the male Betta for his role in the reproductive process, specifically his task of guarding and tending to the newly hatched fry once they emerge from their eggs.

Conversely, the female betta undergoes a more noticeable transformation during the conditioning period. As she is provided with a more abundant and nutrient-rich diet, her belly gradually swells, becoming visibly larger. This phenomenon is a clear indicator of her developing ovarian sac, which begins to fill with eggs. For breeders, this visual cue is invaluable, as it signals that the female is approaching the optimal state for breeding. The swelling of the female's belly is particularly visibled in light-colored specimens, where the translucent nature of their skin allows for a direct view of the ovarian sac's gradual expansion.

The process of conditioning also involves monitoring the overall health and well-being of the betta pair. Breeders pay close attention to any signs of stress, disease, or physical abnormalities. Water quality and environmental conditions are meticulously maintained within their respective tanks to create a stable and comfortable environment for the fish. Temperature, pH levels, and water hardness are closely monitored and adjusted as needed to mimic the ideal conditions found in their natural habitat (we generally raise the temperature to around 82°F and acidify the water slightly to bring it closer to pH 6).

In addition to dietary adjustments and water parameters, breeders may also take other measures to enhance the conditioning of their betta pair. This can include the use of specific vitamins, supplements, or water additives that are believed to promote overall health and reproductive vigor. While these supplements are not always considered mandatory, we may incorporate them into the conditioning regimen to provide every possible advantage to bettas.

Necessary Materials

The second crucial step in the intricate process of betta reproduction involves gathering the necessary materials and setting up the breeding environment. This step is pivotal in ensuring a conducive and controlled environment for the successful breeding. At the heart of this stage lies the careful selection and arrangement of various components within the breeding tank. To initiate the process, you must assemble a minimum set of essential items, including :

- a male betta and a female betta (of course..!)
- a suitable tank or aquarium
- a reliable heater, a thermometer
- hiding spots or shelters for the female betta,
- a structure or support for the bubble nest that the male betta will construct.

These materials collectively create a environement that mimics the natural habitat of Betta splendens, providing a secure and controlled space for the breeding pair to engage in their intricate courtship and reproductive behaviors.

The choice of tank or aquarium is significant, and many breeders opt for "tortoise tanks" due to their dimensions, which are typically around 14 x 10 x 7 inch, providing approximately 4 gallon of water volume. These tanks offer ample floor space, an advantage that becomes crucial during breeding, as it provides both a larger volume of water at equal depth and greater separation between the area designated for bubble nest construction and the space reserved for hiding. Moreover, these tanks are typically placed on a black background, such as felt, which aids in making the white eggs more visible when they fall to the bottom of the tank during spawning.

To ensure the privacy and visual isolation of the breeding pair from other bettas, three of the tank's four sides are often covered with sheets of neoprene foam, allowing for unobstructed viewing from the front and one side. This isolation is essential as it minimizes stress and distractions for the breeding pair, creating an environment conducive to their natural courtship and reproduction behaviors. Additionally, the tank is usually topped with a clear plexiglass cover to prevent drafts and to ensure the adults remain within the confines of the tank, preventing any accidental escapes.

Water quality is of paramount importance during this stage, and breeders often use a combination of methods to create the ideal aquatic environment for bettas. While some breeders may use tap water, even if it is hard and high in mineral content, others opt for softer water conditions achieved through the use of reverse osmosis water (RO) to which various additives are introduced. These additives can include Preiss salts or sea salt, or others like Atison's Betta Spa from Ocean Nutrition, which not only help create water chemistry closer to that of the betta's natural habitat but also enhance the adherence of the bubble nests and the overall health of the breeding pair.

Arrangement

The arrangement of the breeding tank for betta is a critical aspect of ensuring a successful breeding process. This stage involves careful consideration of the tank's interior setup, with a focus on providing essential elements that support the natural behaviors and needs of the breeding pair. One key element is the use of a catappa leaf as a support for the bubble nest. This leaf, preferably an older one that won't release excessive tannins, serves as the foundation upon which the male betta constructs his characteristic bubble nest. The leaf's presence mimics the floating vegetation that male bettas often use as a nest site in the wild, making it an essential component of the tank setup.

In addition to the catappa leaf, breeders commonly introduce other elements to the tank to enhance its suitability for breeding. These include the addition of hiding spots or shelters, such as clay pots laid on their sides or coconut halves, which serve a dual purpose. They provide refuge and privacy for the female betta, allowing her to escape the male's advances if needed, and they also act as ideal hiding places for the fry once they hatch. Another addition is the inclusion of Cladophora, a type of green algae, which not only serves as hiding spots for the female but also acts as a source of infusoria, a tiny live food that can be beneficial for the newly hatched fry during their initial days.

Introduction

First introduce the male betta to the breeding tank. It's a crucial step which must repeat the classic acclimatization steps (page 38). This stage involves a careful transition from the male's regular maintenance tank to the specially prepared breeding environment, ensuring minimal stress and potential injury to the fish. The procedure typically begins by gently capturing the male Betta using a plastic pot or cup, which is then placed in a water bath within the breeding tank. This method allows for a gradual increase in water temperature, matching the conditions of the breeding tank, and avoids the need to use a net, which could potentially damage the male's delicate fins.

This gradual acclimatization process is essential, particularly for Betta varieties with long and delicate finnage, as it minimizes the risk of damage during the transfer. It also eliminates the unnecessary stress of handling and reduces the chances of the male becoming distressed. Once the water temperatures have equilibrated, the male betta is released into the breeding tank, where he begins to adapt to his new surroundings.

After the male's introduction, he is left alone in the tank for a period of 24 to 48 hours. During this time, he can acclimate to the environment, familiarize himself with the territory, and potentially begin constructing the bubble nest. The change in water conditions, transitioning from his maintenance tank to the breeding tank, often triggers the male's instinct to build a bubble nest, a critical step in the breeding process. Elements like the catappa leaf, hiding spots, and water additives play a role in this behavioral shift, promoting the onset of nest construction. This process is monitored closely by the breeder, as the presence of a well-constructed nest signals the male's readiness to receive the female for spawning.

As with the male, the female is harvested and acclimatized in the breeding tank in a separate floating container (a plastic pot or cup). Once the female has acclimated to the tank's environment, she is carefully introduced into the breeding space, often with a protective cloche-like structure for 24 hours. In many cases, breeders use a upside-down plasitc cup with the bottom removed and protruding above the aquarium water level. This allowing the female to remain separate from the male initially. This protective barrier prevents immediate physical contact between the male and female, as it is essential to gauge their readiness and willingness to spawn without risking aggressive encounters or injuries.

During this introductory phase, the male and female are observed closely for specific behavioral cues. A receptive female typically exhibits signs of readiness for spawning, including holding her ground against the approaching male, frenetic swimming near the the cup wall, with vertical striping on her body and sometimes assuming a head-down position. On the other hand, the male entices the female by swimming back and forth between her and the bubble nest, attempting to encourage her to join him beneath the nest. These interactions are good signals for releasing the female into the tank with the male.

The mating

The moment when the female betta is released into the breeding tank is a culmination of careful preparation and observation.

The male's courtship efforts intensify. He becomes a whirlwind of activity, displaying vibrant colors and flaring his fins in an attempt to impress the female. He approaches her with an elaborate dance, enticing her to join him beneath the bubble nest. This courtship dance can appear aggressive to an observer unfamiliar with Betta behavior. The male may chase the female, nipping at her fins and body. This behavior, although seemingly hostile, is a natural part of the courtship process and typically does not result in severe harm to the female.

As the courtship progresses, the male continues to exhibit his vibrant colors and engages in fin displays to capture the female's attention. Once the male successfully guides the female beneath the bubble nest, the culmination of their courtship occurs with the actual act of mating. During this phase, the male wraps his body around the female in a distinctive embrace. This embrace, known as "amplexus," involves the male positioning the female in a way that allows for the simultaneous release and fertilization of her eggs. As they embrace, the female releases her eggs, and the male releases his milt, containing sperm, into the water. The eggs and sperm mix in the surrounding water, ensuring fertilization.

This mating process can be a visually striking spectacle, with the male and female betta intricately intertwined and moving in a synchronized manner. Their colors intensify, creating a breathtaking display. It's important to note that the initial attempts at mating may not always result in the release of eggs. However, with each successive embrace, more eggs are typically expelled and fertilized.

Once the mating is complete, the male resumes his role as the guardian of the nest. He diligently collects the fertilized eggs, securing them in the bubble nest that he has meticulously constructed earlier. This nest-building behavior, characterized by the male creating and maintaining a structure of bubbles at the water's surface, is crucial to protect the vulnerable eggs from potential threats and ensure they receive adequate oxygenation.

As the male retrieves the eggs, he carefully places them within the bubbles of the nest, a process that requires remarkable precision. The female, in the meantime, may appear momentarily motionless after each embrace, allowing the male to perform this critical task without interference. The male's commitment to safeguarding the eggs is unwavering, and he remains vigilant, ensuring that no eggs fall to the bottom of the tank or become dislodged from the nest.

The female's role, on the other hand, evolves after the mating process. While she may continue to stay in the proximity of the male and nest, her interaction with the eggs changes. Some females may display maternal instincts and assist the male in tending to the eggs, while others may exhibit a different behavior pattern. Unfortunately, it's not uncommon for some females to consume the eggs during this phase. This behavior may be influenced by various factors, including the female's individual temperament, experience, and the availability of alternative food sources. It is often at this time that the female is removed from the aquarium to avoid any rivalry with the male who will defend the eggs.

The male stays under the nest, fortifying it from time to time and pulling up any eggs that come loose from the nest. The aquarium light can be left on continuously during incubation.
Should the male lose interest in egg-laying or start eating the eggs, it is advisable to remove him (although he may eat only some of the unfertilized eggs).

Hatching

At 28°, the first fry hatch after around 36 hours.
During the first 48 hours, the fry resorb their yolk sac and swim vertically only. Not always having the energy to return to the bubble nest, they remain dependent on their father, who gobbles them up when they fall out of the nest, before releasing them into the bubble nest or just below.

The first fry swim freely 24 to 36 hours after hatching, the majority by the end of the second day. At this stage, they should be fed live food, ideally to increase survival rates like vinegar eels (Turbatrix aceti), which will remain their main food source for the rest of the first week.

As soon as the first fry are free-swimming, we remove the hiding places and siphon off the waste accumulated at the bottom of the tank to reach a water level of 4 to 5 cm. Depending on how tired he is, the male can be removed at the same time, or a little later (up to 5 days after hatching, with no risk of predation on the fry, although this should be monitored).
The male usually remains under the bubble nest, where he is difficult to retrieve, and can be attracted by placing a mirror against the front window of the tank and retrieving him in a plastic cup or using a landing net. If a few fry are caught at the same time, they should be recovered with a syringe before being released back into the breeding tank.

▲ Various male bettas tending their bubble nest and collecting eggs from the ground.

You now have all the information to get started and take care of your fighting fish. We wish you a lot of fun and many pleasant hours contemplating your new aquarium and its occupant.

And if this guide has helped you, do not hesitate to let us know by leaving an opinion on the comment space accessible below.

Your opinion is important to us

Create review

Also discover our other book, dedicated to the fabulous aquaristic world :

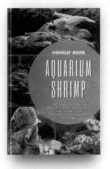

https://www.amazon.com/gp/product/B0BS8SMXD7/

https://www.amazon.com/gp/product/B0CR2P2H7Q

https://www.amazon.com/gp/product/B0CNLW3S1M

See you soon.

PSSSSST !

If you have no experience of aquarium keeping and are about to embark on this wonderful world with the acquisition of a fighting fish, we've thought of you to make your first steps easier!

On the following pages, you'll find maintenance sheets for you to complete for the next 24 weeks. They will guide you through the maintenance tasks to be carried out, and help you keep track of the calendar. This way, you'll know exactly when and which tasks to carry out to keep your fighter's aquarium as healthy and beautiful as your fish !

Care and maintenance

Follow-up sheet ✓

Date : ....

Water checking 💧

Temperature : .... °K   **Nitrites (NO2) :** .... mg/l

PH : ....   **Nitrates (NO3) :** .... mg/l

GH : ....   **Phosphate (PO4) :** .... mg/l

KH : ....   **CO2 / FER :** .... / .... mg/l

---

Water change

% of water changed : ....%   **in gallon** : .... g

Tap water : ....g   **Osmosis water :** .... g

---

Filtration ♻

Cleaning :   Rinsing filter materials ☐

Replacement of filter materials ☐

MY MAINTENANCE SHEET TO
CUT OUT AND STICK ON THE
TANK GLASS SO YOU DON'T
FORGET ANYTHING !

✂ - - - - - - - - - - - - - - - - -

Last maintenance : ....

Next maintenance for : ....

To do :   Filtration ☐   Water change ☐
          Glass ☐   Plants ☐

Care and maintenance

Follow-up sheet

Date : ....

Water checking

Temperature : .... °K   **Nitrites (NO2) :** .... mg/l

PH : ....   **Nitrates (NO3) :** .... mg/l

GH : ....   **Phosphate (PO4) :** .... mg/l

KH : ....   **CO2 / FER :** .... / .... mg/l

Water change

% of water changed : ....%   **in gallon :** .... g

Tap water : .... g   **Osmosis water :** .... g

Filtration

Cleaning :

Rinsing filter materials ☐

Replacement of filter materials ☐

MY MAINTENANCE SHEET TO CUT OUT AND STICK ON THE TANK GLASS SO YOU DON'T FORGET ANYTHING !

Last maintenance : ....

Next maintenance for : ....

To do : Filtration ☐ Water change ☐ Glass ☐ Plants ☐

Care and maintenance

Follow-up sheet

Date : ....

Water checking

Temperature : .... °K   Nitrites (NO2) : .... mg/l

PH : ....   Nitrates (NO3) : .... mg/l

GH : ....   Phosphate (PO4) : .... mg/l

KH : ....   CO2 / FER : .... / .... mg/l

Water change

% of water changed : ....%   in gallon   : .... g

Tap water   : .... g   Osmosis water : .... g

Filtration ♳

Cleaning :

Rinsing filter materials ☐

Replacement of filter materials ☐

MY MAINTENANCE SHEET TO CUT OUT AND STICK ON THE TANK GLASS SO YOU DON'T FORGET ANYTHING !

Last maintenance   : ....

Next maintenance for : ....

To do :   Filtration ☐   Water change ☐

Glass ☐   Plants ☐

Care and maintenance

Follow-up sheet

Date : ....

Water checking

Temperature : .... °K   **Nitrites (NO2) :** .... mg/l

PH : ....   **Nitrates (NO3) :** .... mg/l

GH : ....   **Phosphate (PO4) :** .... mg/l

KH : ....   **CO2 / FER :** .... / .... mg/l

Water change

% of water changed : ....%   **in gallon :** .... g

Tap water : .... g   **Osmosis water :** .... g

Filtration

Cleaning :   Rinsing filter materials ☐

   Replacement of filter materials ☐

MY MAINTENANCE SHEET TO CUT OUT AND STICK ON THE TANK GLASS SO YOU DON'T FORGET ANYTHING !

Last maintenance : ....

Next maintenance for : ....

To do :   Filtration ☐   Water change ☐

   Glass ☐   Plants ☐

Care and maintenance

Follow-up sheet ☑

Date : ....

Water checking 💧

Temperature : .... °K   **Nitrites (NO2) :** .... mg/l

PH : ....   **Nitrates (NO3) :** .... mg/l

GH : ....   **Phosphate (PO4) :** .... mg/l

KH : ....   **CO2 / FER :** .... / .... mg/l

Water change

% of water changed : ....%   **in gallon :** .... g

Tap water : .... g   **Osmosis water :** .... g

Filtration ♻

Cleaning :   Rinsing filter materials ☐

Replacement of filter materials ☐

MY MAINTENANCE SHEET TO CUT OUT AND STICK ON THE TANK GLASS SO YOU DON'T FORGET ANYTHING !

Last maintenance : ....

Next maintenance for : ....

To do :   Filtration ☐   Water change ☐   Glass ☐   Plants ☐

Care and maintenance

Follow-up sheet

Date : ....

Water checking

Temperature : .... °K   **Nitrites (NO2) :** .... mg/l

PH : ....   **Nitrates (NO3) :** .... mg/l

GH : ....   **Phosphate (PO4) :** .... mg/l

KH : ....   **CO2 / FER :** .... / .... mg/l

Water change

% of water changed : .... %   **in gallon :** .... g

Tap water : .... g   **Osmosis water :** .... g

Filtration ♺

Cleaning :   Rinsing filter materials   ☐

Replacement of filter materials   ☐

MY MAINTENANCE SHEET TO CUT OUT AND STICK ON THE TANK GLASS SO YOU DON'T FORGET ANYTHING !

Last maintenance : ....

Next maintenance for : ....

To do :   Filtration ☐   Water change ☐
          Glass ☐   Plants ☐

Care and maintenance

Follow-up sheet 📋

Date : ....

Water checking 💧

Temperature : .... °K	**Nitrites (NO2) :** .... mg/l
PH :	**Nitrates (NO3) :** .... mg/l
GH :	**Phosphate (PO4) :** .... mg/l
KH :	**CO2 / FER :** .... / .... mg/l

---

Water change

% of water changed : .... %   **in gallon** : .... g

Tap water : .... g   **Osmosis water :** .... g

---

Filtration ♻️

Cleaning :

Rinsing filter materials ☐

Replacement of filter materials ☐

MY MAINTENANCE SHEET TO
CUT OUT AND STICK ON THE
TANK GLASS SO YOU DON'T
FORGET ANYTHING !

Last maintenance : ....

Next maintenance for : ....

To do :   Filtration ☐   Water change ☐

Glass ☐   Plants ☐

Care and maintenance

Date : ....

Follow-up sheet 📋

Water checking 💧

Temperature : .... °K   **Nitrites (NO2) :** .... mg/l

PH : ....   **Nitrates (NO3) :** .... mg/l

GH : ....   **Phosphate (PO4) :** .... mg/l

KH : ....   **CO2 / FER :** .... / .... mg/l

Water change

% of water changed : .... %   **in gallon :** .... g

Tap water : .... g   **Osmosis water :** .... g

Filtration ♻

Cleaning :   Rinsing filter materials   ☐

                        Replacement of filter materials   ☐

MY MAINTENANCE SHEET TO
CUT OUT AND STICK ON THE
TANK GLASS SO YOU DON'T
FORGET ANYTHING !

| Last maintenance : .... |
| Next maintenance for : .... |

To do :   Filtration ☐   Water change ☐
            Glass ☐   Plants ☐

Care and maintenance

Follow-up sheet 📋

Date : ....

💧 Water checking

Temperature : .... °K	**Nitrites (NO2) :** .... mg/l
PH :	**Nitrates (NO3) :** .... mg/l
GH :	**Phosphate (PO4) :** .... mg/l
KH :	**CO2 / FER :** .... / .... mg/l

Water change

% of water changed : ....%   **in gallon**   : .... g

Tap water   : .... g   **Osmosis water :** .... g

Filtration ♺

Cleaning :   Rinsing filter materials ☐

   Replacement of filter materials ☐

MY MAINTENANCE SHEET TO CUT OUT AND STICK ON THE TANK GLASS SO YOU DON'T FORGET ANYTHING !

Last maintenance   : ....

Next maintenance for : ....

To do :   Filtration ☐   Water change ☐
       Glass ☐   Plants ☐

Care and maintenance

Follow-up sheet

Date : ....

Water checking

Temperature : .... °K   **Nitrites (NO2) :** .... mg/l

PH : ....   **Nitrates (NO3) :** .... mg/l

GH : ....   **Phosphate (PO4) :** .... mg/l

KH : ....   **CO2 / FER :** ..../........ mg/l

Water change

% of water changed : ....% **in gallon** : .... g

Tap water : ....g **Osmosis water :** .... g

Filtration

Cleaning :

Rinsing filter materials ☐

Replacement of filter materials ☐

MY MAINTENANCE SHEET TO CUT OUT AND STICK ON THE TANK GLASS SO YOU DON'T FORGET ANYTHING !

Last maintenance : ....

Next maintenance for : ....

To do : Filtration ☐ Water change ☐

Glass ☐ Plants ☐

Care and maintenance

Follow-up sheet

Date : ....

Water checking

Temperature : .... °K   **Nitrites (NO2) :** .... mg/l

      PH : ....   **Nitrates (NO3) :** .... mg/l

      GH : ....   **Phosphate (PO4) :** .... mg/l

      KH : ....   **CO2 / FER :** .... / .... mg/l

---

Water change

% of water changed : .... %   **in gallon**   : .... g

Tap water   : .... g   **Osmosis water :** .... g

---

Filtration ♻

                Rinsing filter materials   ☐

Cleaning :

                Replacement of filter materials   ☐

MY MAINTENANCE SHEET TO
CUT OUT AND STICK ON THE
TANK GLASS SO YOU DON'T
FORGET ANYTHING !

Last maintenance   : ....

Next maintenance for : ....

To do :   Filtration ☐   Water change ☐

        Glass ☐   Plants ☐

Care and maintenance

Follow-up sheet ✅

Date : ....

Water checking 💧

Temperature : .... °K	**Nitrites (NO2) :** .... mg/l
PH :	**Nitrates (NO3) :** .... mg/l
GH :	**Phosphate (PO4) :** .... mg/l
KH :	**CO2 / FER :** .... / .... mg/l

---

Water change

% of water changed : ....%   **in gallon**   **:** .... g

Tap water   **:** .... g   **Osmosis water :** .... g

---

Filtration ♻

Cleaning :

Rinsing filter materials ☐

Replacement of filter materials ☐

MY MAINTENANCE SHEET TO
CUT OUT AND STICK ON THE
TANK GLASS SO YOU DON'T
FORGET ANYTHING !

Last maintenance : ....

Next maintenance for : ....

To do :   Filtration ☐   Water change ☐
      Glass ☐   Plants ☐

Made in the USA
Columbia, SC
17 December 2024